The 21st-Century Principal

D1606527

Current Issues in Leadership and Policy

edited by **Milli Pierce**
and **Deborah L. Stapleton**

HARVARD EDUCATION PRESS

Library of Congress Control Number 2002111700
ISBN 1-891792-06-7

Published by Harvard Education Press,
an imprint of the Harvard Education Publishing Group

Harvard Education Press
8 Story Street, 5th Floor
Cambridge, MA 02138

Cover Design: Kate Canfield
Editorial Production: Dody Riggs
Typography: Sheila Walsh

The typefaces used in this book are Bitstream Kuenstler 480 and Humanist 777.

Contents

Preface

Seldom do we set out to mine gold and actually end up excavating a product of profound richness. Yet the conversations that make up this volume—which were edited and adapted from transcripts of lectures and discussions at a two-day Principals' Center institute entitled *Leadership and Policy: An Education Forum*—are just such a product.

More than 200 principals met in November 2001 to consider the views of a distinguished faculty and to debate for themselves some of the most important issues that will affect their profession in the coming decades. Panelists and participants alike unraveled such topics as the purposes of public education, standards and accountability, the impact of privatization and choice on public schools, and the black/white achievement gap.

The following chapters deliver imaginative, thoughtful discussions of these issues and more, based on the research and expertise of our presenters. Unlike traditional academic essays, these offerings are conversation starters intended to spark further discussion in your own school and district. Together they function as a kind of workbook to help you sort out the local impact of global issues.

As you explore this book, you will undoubtedly have strong opinions about some of the ideas you encounter. You will likely agree enthusiastically with some and disagree vehemently with others. To facilitate conversation in your own work environments, we have provided discussion questions at the end of each chapter. We hope these questions provoke a lively exchange of answers, inspire more questions, and stimulate a discussion within your community that is as rich as the one the institute participants enjoyed.

Milli Pierce
Deborah L. Stapleton

Introduction:
The 21st-Century Principal

Milli Pierce

> "There is always a choice about the way you
> do your work, even if there is not a choice
> about the work itself."
>> —*Stephen Lundin, business coach and author*

The essays in this volume examine the future of public
schooling in the United States—and what it will
mean to be a leader in public schools—by focusing on
the issues that are most likely to have an impact on
American society within the next 20 years. Like so many
other things, public schooling is deeply affected by context.
As the context of schooling changes, principals will need to
refocus their work so that schools can change in accordance
with the populations they serve.

Some of the most dramatic changes in the context of
schooling are demographic. As Harold Hodgkinson reminds

us in chapter three, "The Challenge of a Changing Nation," senior citizens are a burgeoning population. Soon there will be many states whose demographics resemble the current population of Florida. Senior citizens are living longer, healthier, and more active lives. Hodgkinson notes that by the year 2025, at least 20 percent of the citizens in more than 27 states will be over the age of 65. Public school advocates might well be concerned about the fact that the children of these older citizens are having fewer children, which means fewer senior citizens will be grandparents. Why would seniors who have no grandchildren and who are concerned about their own health benefits, Social Security, and pensions be inclined to support public schools, particularly if those schools have reputations for being ineffective? What will this changing demographic mean for public education? Principals need to consider these kinds of questions as they look ahead.

We live in one of the wealthiest nations in the world, yet the number of poor children is increasing. At least 20 percent of the children in this country under the age of 18 are living in poverty, and that number is on the rise. We are becoming a country divided more by class than by race, as the have-nots outnumber the haves. Children from these poorest families live in all kinds of places, including some you might not expect. For example, the largest pockets of poverty are in rural America. In Oklahoma, 32 percent of children live in poverty, as do 16 percent of Vermont's children. Large pockets of children both in cities and in rural areas hidden from public view live in poverty. What will this mean for public education?

Being a principal means being part of the decisionmaking process about how to handle the big challenges ahead of us.

How will we educate every child to a high standard? How will we convince senior citizens to vote their own interests and the children's interests as well? Whose job will it be to convince them to do that?

THE CHANGING ROLE OF THE PRINCIPAL

In the coming decades, principals will need to take on an ever larger role in the work of convincing the public to support public schools. Teacher unions will also have to play a substantive role in convincing the public of our schools' value and importance. Failure to do so may put them out of business.

It is clear that traditional public schools will either respond to the children and communities they serve, or they will be replaced by charter schools, parochial schools, and private academies. Support for these alternatives will probably take the form of vouchers, and possibly tax credits. If we cannot make schools responsive to the children who need them and to the citizens who provide tax revenues, we may indeed lose our right to public education.

Public education is intended for all children, but some policy analysts predict that if public schools fail to improve dramatically, the only students served there will be those who have nowhere else to go. Everyone else is going to pull out and put their children in independent schools. We must work to guarantee that all children have the chance to achieve to a high standard. We already have plenty of evidence to suggest that if children are failing to meet state standards, parents will take them elsewhere. Furthermore, as fewer people are choosing to have children, we cannot expect their concerns to mirror ours. What will become of public education if we cannot provide a reason for its existence to all taxpayers, not just those with children? They will insist on putting their tax dollars where they think they will make the most difference.

One of the questions we should be asking ourselves is, do we care enough to improve our schools? If we do care, how will we get the work done? One way to ensure success is to hold principals accountable, to have them hire and give them the right to fire. In most of the worst schools, principals are sent teachers without the benefit of refusal, and this must change. The primary focus of any reform effort should be on the quality of instruction. That is the bottom line. There is no more time for excuses.

INSISTING ON QUALITY

What does quality instruction look like? We want to create lifelong learners. We want knowledgeable and caring teachers. We must attend to all different kinds of students and be prepared to address individual needs. We should teach values and model what it means to be moral human beings. We should teach children how to learn and how to access information. We should teach the arts to children and help them learn to cooperate with one another. We should teach and demonstrate good citizenship. We should provide safe places for students and teachers to take risks. We want children involved in the planning of their learning, and parents must be more involved as well. Schools can be places where community interests can be woven together, where the fabric of a community can be made stronger. We want a place that prepares students to be productive citizens with a wide range of talents and skills.

If we want parents to be an integral part of the school community, we must make them feel comfortable there. The notion of expanding the idea of schools to be community centers takes on greater importance as we welcome greater numbers of immigrants. The missions of the community and of schools become intertwined.

We also need to have leaders with foresight who can plan five to ten years out. How will we support schools and attract the best people to work in them? There are no teachers, beginning or senior, who earn what a beginning attorney in a medium-sized firm earns in Boston. These young people fresh out of law school are earning $150,000 a year, compared to a beginning teacher who earns around $30,000 a year. If the world tells us that teaching is important, then we must behave as if it *were* important by rewarding those who do the work well.

We need excellence and equity. We need collaboration and cooperation. We need a structure in education that can attract excellence. We need a greater connection between social policy and educational policy. How do we connect social policy or policymaking to what's actually happening in the schools? Why do principals and teachers feel left out of policymaking?

We should all be concerned about educating our children. Policy analysts must realize that their concerns are not different from those of educators. Major education policy must be enacted only after hearing the voices of those entrusted with doing the work. How will we recruit new teachers and principals if aspirants believe they will be left out of the decision-making process for their own workplace?

THE FUTURE OF THE PRINCIPAL'S PROFESSION

Forty percent of our principals will retire in the next three years. How will we rebuild this work force? Will current principals and teachers be advocates for this work? It takes a concurrent effort on the part of teachers and principals to attract the best people to the profession. Everybody who believes schools are worth having and saving must work together to enlist the next generation of teachers and principal leaders to make this work force strong and viable.

We're asking our 21st-century principals to do more and more, and the job is becoming one that few people want. You only have to look at the statistics across the United States. As principals are retiring, people are not standing at school employment offices saying, "Please take me! I want to be a principal." There's a reason for that. The job is becoming more difficult, the hours are getting longer, and we cannot expect people to sacrifice their personal lives so that they can spend as many as 80 hours a week in school. The high-end pay for a principal is about $90,000. You do the math.

For principals to remain in this work they will need to be skilled at creating strong, committed teams. This means that they need to be strong instructional leaders and need to develop teacher leaders who can help them run the school. These teachers will help manage the school, handle the budget, keep the buses running on time. If principals are expected to do it all we can be assured of mediocre performance, not because they aren't capable but because we have asked them to be superhuman, because we do not provide the professional development time they need to learn new skills. Many principals also serve without assistance. A principal in a school of 2,000 might have an assistant principal, but in a school of 600, chances are the principal is running the school alone. Under these conditions, should we be surprised that, when forced to choose a role, many principals say the manager wins out over the instructional leader?

SCHOOL: A PLACE OF HOPES AND DREAMS

I would argue that the mission of a school is framed around hopes and dreams. Once we start extinguishing these with policies, restrictions, and a lack of resources, then we're really denying kids their dreams.

This year's kindergartners will be with us for the next 13 years. If we go back 13 years and look at the world then—when we were fumbling around with CDs that were just coming out, when we were still talking about a divided Germany—we realize how much things can change while students are a part of our lives. Who among us can predict what will happen 13 years from *now*? What world will today's five-year-olds be facing when they graduate at age 18? They must be equipped with hopes and dreams, and it's incumbent upon us to create environments in the context of this changing world that will nurture and cultivate these aspirations.

1

The Limits of Change

Richard F. Elmore

Richard F. Elmore, Gregory R. Anrig Professor of Educational Leadership at the Harvard Graduate School of Education, draws the important distinction between school change and school improvement. In far too many schools, Elmore says, change often takes the form of the latest structural "reform du jour" with little consideration as to whether it will actually result in improved student learning. According to Elmore, meaningful reform happens only when structural changes are aligned with improvement goals from the start and schools have the organization in place to meet the demands of accountability.

For the last 15 years, I have been studying the "geological accumulation" of education reforms in U.S. schools—the sedimentation of the last two or three geological eras of school reform. In a book I wrote with Penelope Peterson and Sarah McCarthey on the structure and restructuring of schools, the main finding we report is that changing structure does not change practice. In fact, the schools that seem to do the best are those that have a clear idea of what kind of instructional practice they want to produce, and then design a structure to go with it.

My favorite story, which is now increasingly confirmed by the aggregate analysis of block scheduling—the current structural "reform du jour" of secondary education—involves a high school social studies teacher I interviewed recently. I asked him, "So what do you think of block scheduling?" He said, "It's the best thing that's ever happened in my teaching career." I asked, "Why?" And he replied, "Now we can show the whole movie."

That captures my take on structural reform. We put an enormous amount of energy into changing structures and usually leave instructional practice untouched. That message has certainly been confirmed by Fred Newmann's work at the Center on Organization and Restructuring of Schools and other research. We are just getting the results of the first generation of aggregate studies on block scheduling, which, shockingly, show no relationship between its adoption and any outcome that you can measure on student performance. Of course, this is exactly what one could have predicted, given the previous research on structural reforms.

Notice that I didn't say structural changes don't matter. They often matter a lot, especially when you're talking about

U.S. high schools, which are probably a close third or tied for second as the most pathological social institutions in our society, after public health hospitals and prisons. There are problems in high schools that cannot be solved without making dramatic changes in structure, but in the vast number of cases there is no instrumental relationship between any change in structure, any change in practice, and any change in student performance. That is the big problem with the usual approaches to school improvement. We are viscerally and instinctively inclined to move the boxes around on the organizational chart, to fiddle with the schedule. We are attracted and drawn to these things largely because they're visible and, believe it or not, easier to do than to make the hard changes, which are in instructional practice.

The pathology of U.S. schools is that they know how to change. They know how to change promiscuously and at the drop of a hat. What schools do not know how to do is to improve, to engage in sustained and continuous progress toward a performance goal over time. So the task is to develop practice around the notion of improvement.

We can talk about what's wrong with the state accountability systems that are springing up everywhere, but the fact is that school improvement strategies are being driven by performance-based accountability systems. These systems involve setting standards for what constitutes good practice, a solid curriculum, and acceptable student performance. They entail various kinds of stakes for students and for schools—and virtually none for teachers and administrators.

The problem, however, is that the organizations we work in aren't designed to respond to this kind of performance pressure. We may know what to do theoretically, but I have serious doubts that we know what to do at the level of practice. For example, I've been in enough high school math classes over the last five years to know that there is no developmental theory of how students learn algebra. The kids who don't make it and don't respond to the kind of instruction they're receiving are simply not included in the instructional model. Furthermore, teachers in the classrooms I've observed take no responsibility for the lowest-performing students, because the prevailing theory suggests that learning mathematics is not a developmental problem but a problem of aptitude. Some people get it, some don't. (In this regard, literacy is perhaps an exception.)

Many teachers do not believe that learning problems can be solved by inquiry, by evidence, and by science. They do not believe that it is necessary to have a developmental theory of how students learn the content or how the pedagogy relates to the development of knowledge and content. Nor are most teachers interested in addressing the intellectual and professional challenge that some of their students will learn the content and some will not. As a result, we are asking schools to make improvements in the presence of an extremely weak technical core.

Also, schools are not organized to support problem-solving based on cooperation or collaboration. The ethic of atomized teaching—teachers practicing as individuals with individual styles—is very strong in U.S. schools. We subscribe to a peculiar view of professionalism; that is, that professionalism equals autonomy in practice. So when I go to a classroom and ask, "Why are you teaching in this way?" it is often viewed as a violation of the teacher's autonomy and professionalism.

Consider what would happen if you were on an airplane and the pilot came on the intercom as you were about to start your descent and said, "I've always wanted to try this without the flaps." Or if your cardiovascular surgeon said to you in your presurgical conference, "You know, I'd really like to do this the way I originally learned to do it in 1978." Would you be a willing participant in either case?

Of course, in the "real" professions people get sued for such behavior, as the absence of a strong technical core of knowledge and discourse about what effective practice is carries a very high price. However, in the teaching profession, we know what works instructionally in many content areas, but the distribution of knowledge is uneven, and we resist the idea of calibrating our practice to external benchmarks or knowledge bases.

School systems are also characterized by weak internal accountability. When I use that term, I mean the intersection between the individual's sense of responsibility, the organization's expectations about what constitutes quality instruction and good student performance, and the systemic means or processes by which we actually account for what we do. How frequently do we observe teachers? How do we analyze performance data? How do we think about teachers' performance? The schools in which these factors are aligned have powerful approaches to improving instruction. When they are not aligned—and in most cases they are not—schools have extreme difficulty responding to external pressure for improved performance.

Meanwhile, the usual remediation strategy we employ when kids fail to meet statewide testing requirements is to give them the same unbelievably bad instruction they got in the first place, only in much larger quantities with much greater intensity. This is what we call the louder and slower approach.

This brings me back to the notion of improvement versus the notion of change. Improvement is a discipline. It requires picking a target that has something to do with demonstrated student learning, one that's ambitious enough to put schools in an improvement mode. If you're a school leader whose students are scoring consistently in the 95th percentile, you need another performance measure because that one is doing you no good, except perhaps to help your marketing. To measure any improvement you need a new ceiling, a goal to push for that's quite a distance from where you are. You also need some kind of external benchmarks.

If the only benchmarks you have come from your own connoisseurship—your particular opinions and ideas about what good practice is—then you're in trouble. Real improvement comes when you visit a classroom where somebody is doing the same thing you are—only much better. That's when the real conversation, the tough conversation about improvement, takes place. Whether you're a novice or an expert, the important thing is to focus on the next stage of improvement and to determine where that increment of knowledge and skill is going to come from.

For example, it is important for high school educators to understand developmental differences in how students approach basic academic content. There are a large number of high school students for whom reading means reading the text and reporting on facts. A vast proportion of these kids attend decent high schools and are doing reasonably well. Their performance, however, is actually concealed by state-level tests. If you ask them to write an interpretive essay, they simply cannot do it because they've never been taken from merely prying facts out of a text to understanding, interpreting, and adding meaning to it. And while this is a significant problem in literacy and reading, it's a much larger problem in mathematics. A large number of students have no relationship to mathematical knowledge whatsoever, and the remediation strategies that we discuss and use are failing the children and failing to meet statewide testing requirements.

The norms and values that accompany ambitious conceptions of learning and improvement grow out of practice, not vice versa. School improvement doesn't happen by getting the entire staff to gather in the auditorium and testify to the belief that all children can learn—not if it means sending everyone back to the classroom to do what they've always done. Only a change in practice produces a genuine change in norms and values. Or, to put it more crudely, grab people by their practice and their hearts and minds will follow.

Finally, the practice of improvement involves the creation of strong internal accountability systems. It's David Hawkins' "I, thou, and it" framework—the teacher, the student, the content. You have instruction only when you have a teacher and a student engaged in common work around a body of content. So, if you think you can achieve high-quality instruction by giving teachers generic advice about their teaching that's disconnected from content, you're probably not going to have much of an impact on practice and on performance. To achieve high-quality instruction, you first need to know what teachers actually know about the content. Teachers have to know about what they're teaching in order to teach it well. We must work on raising our expectations about the level at which students are expected to learn. This is usually represented in how we understand content and at what level we aim to teach it. And we must work on the skills and knowledge students need in order to be engaged in high-level instruction.

If we are going to make improvement the main task of leadership, then school leaders are going to need to develop that practice in three domains. First, we need to know and to model what kinds of knowledge people need to do this work: knowledge about performance, about development in content areas, about the improvement of instructional skills, and about how to create structures for the way people learn in schools.

Second, we have to begin to understand the issue of incentives. A deep understanding of improvement requires a deep understanding of what motivates teachers to teach better and what motivates students to learn at higher levels.

And, finally, we need to take a hard line on the issue of resources and capacity. We should not give schools or school systems another penny to increase their capacity until they can demonstrate that they've spent every single available dollar of their core budget on this problem. We have to start requiring schools to use existing resources. Then we can put money on top of that, because that is the only way to know that the money is being spent productively. Unfortunately, most school leaders don't want to hear that message.

SUGGESTED QUESTIONS TO BEGIN DISCUSSION

1. Has your school or district implemented any structural changes recently? If so, have the links to improvement been clear?

2. Is it ever justifiable to change school structures without a clear sense that the changes are likely to improve student learning? If so, under what circumstances might this be the case?

3. Do you agree with Elmore that schools tend to have "weak internal accountability," especially with regard to what individual teachers teach? If so, how could that situation be changed?

4. Elmore calls for principals to understand what motivates teachers. What do you believe are the primary factors that motivate teachers? What do you believe are the implications of these factors for student achievement?

2

The Six Principles of
Effective Accountability

Douglas B. Reeves

The current national drive toward standards and accountability has caused many educators to implement accountability-based reforms in their own districts. While some of these reform initiatives will succeed, others are bound to fail because they don't take a holistic approach to accountability, says Douglas B. Reeves, chairman and founder of the Center for Performance Assessment and the International Center for Educational Accountability. The real purpose of any accountability system, Reeves says, is the improvement of teaching and learning. However, systems too often focus instead on "excuses," "test scores," "statistical guesses," and other fac-

tors as ends in themselves. Here Reeves outlines what he sees as the six principles of effective accountability.

PRINCIPLE NO. 1: CONGRUENCE

Objectives and strategies are sometimes developed in complete contravention to what the accountability system calls for. Accountability must be the unifying theme that draws strategy, rewards, recognition, and personnel evaluations together.

I once worked in a district that planned to focus its accountability system on the principle of prioritized standards—that is, to focus on the most important standards rather than trying to cover everything at once. That was the rhetoric. But the first line of the teacher evaluation form was, "Did the teacher cover the curriculum?"

In another district, accountability-minded educators said, "We look at the evidence. We know that if more children are involved in extracurricular activities, our attendance and student achievement will be better." Yet when you looked at the recognition and reward system in that district, the teachers they rewarded and recognized were the most exclusive, the ones who protected their classes and their extracurricular activities from any students other than the cream of the crop. In both of these cases, the accountability system was contradicted by the objectives and strategies.

PRINCIPLE NO. 2: SPECIFICITY

If I go to one more conference where we hold hands and chant, "All children can learn," I'm not going to be able to take it anymore. I believe that all children can learn, but I have never achieved anything with a mantra. Accountability is not about chanting mantras; it's not about generalities.

We've got to know specifically what works. We've got to investigate which strategies in our own communities are specifically associated with improved student achievement. And we have to focus on behaviors, not just test scores. In other words, measure what the *grownups* do. We need to set as many standards for the adults—the board members, the administrators, the teachers, perhaps someday even the parents—as we do for the kids.

PRINCIPLE NO. 3: RELEVANCE

There ought to be a direct relationship between the strategies schools employ and improvements in student learning. Of course, relevance isn't always obvious. Some research indicates that, with the exception of attendance, the number-one factor associated with improved test scores and behaviors in the classroom is more nonfiction writing.

It may be obvious that more nonfiction writing is related to better writing scores, and it may make sense that more nonfiction writing is highly related to better reading scores. Less obvious is the fact that even a little more nonfiction writing in a curriculum is also related to better math, science, and social studies scores. In these instances, we find specific relationships between our classroom strategies and our results.

Do these relationships prove causality? Not necessarily. But they do provide us with a way of testing the hypothesis that more nonfiction writing will improve test scores and student behavior. If I were to ask every teacher, "Why can't you do more nonfiction writing?" many would say, "I don't have the time." Time, time, time is the number-one issue. These teachers are articulating the hypothesis that if they spent more time on writing, they wouldn't be able to cover the curriculum, and that would make scores go down. I may not have been able to prove causality, but I have disproved that hypothesis.

PRINCIPLE NO. 4: RESPECT FOR DIVERSITY

"All children can learn" does not mean, "all children are the same." Furthermore, diversity is not merely about external characteristics. If we're really going to take this seriously, that means we start looking at diversity on the inside as well as diversity on the outside. To make this principle both a moral and an intellectual part of the curriculum will require taking different approaches in different schools. That is, it will require diverse approaches, diverse techniques, and diverse teaching strategies.

When U.S. Secretary of Education Rod Paige was running Houston's public schools, he did not say, "My way or the highway" to 200 schools. He said, "You want respect for diversity, including different styles, approaches, and strategies? You've got it. But the price of freedom is transparency. The price of trying different things is being able to come to one another, and to come to me, with transparent results. Tell me what worked, tell me what didn't work." That's what accountability requires. You can embrace different strategies provided you report those strategies. Win or lose, succeed or fail, we report them.

It's important to remember that respecting diversity doesn't mean accepting anarchy or that all views are equal. You can respect diversity without giving up foundational principles. We have the ability, maybe even the mandate, to say that some values are better. The values of freedom, truth, and justice are better than the values of oppression and totalitarianism. That's the kind of thing we ought to be able to say. Not every principle is up for grabs.

PRINCIPLE NO. 5: CONTINUOUS IMPROVEMENT

Jeff Howard, president of the Efficacy Institute, uses an analogy that may resonate for people who have kids. He calls it the Nintendo Effect, which refers to the child who cannot focus or concentrate and is always moving about the classroom until you turn on the Nintendo machine, whereupon the child is transfixed, moving not a follicle of hair as he sits for hours in front of the machine.

The question Dr. Howard asks is, "How long would that child be staring at the screen if you mailed his Nintendo scores to him nine weeks hence?" What keeps him engaged is not just what's happening on the screen, but also the feedback he gets that is timely, immediate, and relevant. If we're going to build a holistic accountability system, once-a-year feedback is not sufficient. We should be building a system that gives feedback every month to our children, our leaders, and our teachers so we can get busy building better instructional systems.

PRINCIPLE NO. 6: FOCUS ON ACHIEVEMENT, NOT NORMS

There is a U.S. state where the Board of Education actually voted that 80 percent of students must be above average. Now, I have taught statistics for a long time, and no amount of listening to Garrison Keillor will convince me that that is a possible distribution. But there's another issue here. When you hear students compared to norms or averages, the normal visceral reaction is that this is something that hurts poor kids. However true that might be, it also hurts advantaged kids.

The bell curve is insidious for *all* kids. It is an ineffective, inappropriate way to measure student achievement. You've got some "above average" kids who are inappropriately complacent and who are hurt by norms as surely as kids who are at the low end of the bell curve. Do you know the 55th-percentile kid who gets a 55th-percentile score in reading and cannot write an essay to save his soul? The 55th-percentile student in math who cannot apply the algorithm in different contexts? The only thing that really matters is whether students are meeting expectations that are clear, objective, and immutable—not who beat whom.

I am suggesting that we have to think about accountability in a very different way. We have done a splendid job in this country of holding nine-year-olds accountable. Let me suggest as a moral principle that we dare not hold kids any more accountable than we expect to hold ourselves.

EFFECTIVE ACCOUNTABILITY:
A MINI-TEST FOR ADMINISTRATORS

Envision yourself in this position. The school nurse comes to you and says, "Bad news, boss. Our accountability system reveals that 44 percent of the kids do not have their required vaccinations. What shall we do?" Do you:

A. fire the school nurse?
B. publish a story in the newspaper to embarrass and humiliate the Health Department about its vaccination program?
C. conduct a five-year study of the vaccination standards and curriculum?
D. gather the data but do not publish it, lest it become a public relations nightmare for the school?
E. get the kids vaccinated?

Most administrators pass this test and answer "E." And even if I use a different analogy—for example, if 44 percent of our school cafeterias were not meeting hygiene standards—most people would still answer "E." It's not a very controversial response.

But if I change vaccinations or cafeteria hygiene to reading or mathematics, how frequently do we leap to A, B, C, or D rather than directly addressing the problem? People who work in secondary education know the fate that befalls students who do not succeed. Statistically, there is a greater health risk for a child who drops out of school than for one who is not vaccinated.

This leads us to a discussion of how accountability can be applied appropriately. What was the purpose of the vaccination report? Was it merely a PR effort, or was its purpose to improve the health of our kids? What, by analogy, should be the purpose of educational accountability? The appropriate response is to improve learning and teaching—period. It is not to break ranks or humiliate anyone. It is not to provide good fodder for the media. Its one and only purpose is to improve student achievement.

—*Douglas B. Reeves*

SUGGESTED QUESTIONS TO BEGIN DISCUSSION

1. Compare the six principles to the accountability system(s) your school or district has used in the past several years. Do any of the principles strike you as especially applicable to your situation? Do any seem irrelevant? Why?

2. According to Reeves, feedback must be "timely, immediate, and relevant." Do you agree? Has your district or school faced any situation where slow feedback has hampered the effectiveness of accountability efforts? If so, are there ways this might have been avoided?

3. Reeves states that norms and comparisons serve little purpose in evaluating student achievement. Do you believe this is true across the board? Or are there exceptions in which comparing students against norms provides useful information?

4. Reeves says, "We dare not hold kids any more accountable than we expect to hold ourselves." Do you believe that we adults hold ourselves accountable? Are there situations you have encountered in which you believe this kind of double standard was a problem?

5. Read the sidebar called "Effective Accountability: A Mini-Test for Administrators." Do you agree with Reeves that "accountability" efforts often lead to blaming, hiding, or long, drawn-out studies that outlive their usefulness? Share any stories you may have in which any of these scenarios have occurred.

3

The Challenge
of a Changing Nation

Marcelo M. Suárez-Orozco

See responses from Harold L. Hodgkinson (p. 35)
and Robert J. Murphy (p. 38)

Our communities are being transformed by globalization, im-
migration, and changing demographic patterns of race and
class. Marcelo M. Suárez-Orozco, Victor S. Thomas Professor
of Education and codirector of the Harvard Immigration Pro-
ject at the Harvard Graduate School of Education, empha-
sizes the importance of considering the trends that will trans-
form the future. What a principal needs to do and needs to
know will change over time, as will the challenges of large-
scale reform, says Suárez-Orozco. He outlines three elements

of globalization that will reshape education in post-industrial democracies.

The first element in the structure of globalization is that economies are increasingly transnational rather than local. From the time you woke up this morning to the time you go to bed tonight, a trillion dollars will have crossed national boundaries. This has profound implications for understanding everything from the way we work to the kinds of things that children will need to know to participate in this increasingly globalized economy.

The second element is the emergence of new information and communications technologies. These too will reshape how we work, how we think, and the social process of cultural life. Maybe it's true that not every kid needs to know trigonometry. But I assure you that the income gaps that we have witnessed in the postindustrial democracies over the last ten or 20 years are precisely predicated on children having had access to the kinds of skills that will be required in economies dominated by knowledge-intensive information technologies.

The third aspect of globalization that will change what we need to do in schools is immigration and migration. There are 100 million transnational migrants, people moving from one country to another. In China there are roughly 100 million internal migrants. In Amsterdam, immigrants will soon make up half of the population. Leicester, England, will soon be the first city in Europe with a non-white majority. Germany, which doesn't think of itself as a country of immigrants, has an immigration rate that is roughly equivalent to the U.S. rate. Frankfurt's population today is one-quarter immigrants.

In the United States, we are now in the middle of the largest wave of immigration in the country's history. The U.S. is becoming the first postindustrial democracy where so-called ethnically marked populations—racial and ethnic minority populations—will in just two generations become roughly half the total population. For example, there will be roughly 100 million people in the United States who trace their descent to the Spanish-speaking Latin American and Caribbean worlds. That will make the United States the second-largest Hispanic country after Mexico.

Globalization is the reason why immigrant children are the fastest-growing sector of the U.S. child population, and this is transforming schools, cities, neighborhoods, and places of work. Roughly one in five children in the U.S. today comes from an immigrant home.

What do we know about what's happening to these kids in schools? In fact, we know very little because few studies include longitudinal data about immigrant students. However, we do know that immigrant children are doing better than ever before in the history of our country. They are overrepresented among the winners of the most prestigious science awards and competitions. They are overrepresented in terms of getting accepted to good colleges. They are bypassing the traditional transgenerational modes of mobility that we've seen in previous waves of immigration.

I coteach a course at Harvard called Latino Culture. We have approximately 150 students. At the first lecture, I asked how many students were immigrants or the children of immigrants. Two-thirds of the students raised their hands. One hundred years ago I would not have been a professor at Harvard University, and two-thirds of any class at Harvard College would not have been from an Eastern European, Italian, or Irish immigrant background.

Yet while many immigrant children are thriving, others are facing dubious odds in the long term. They are going to end up unschooled. They are going to drop out of school and perhaps come under the supervision of the criminal justice system in numbers that we have never seen before. Many are going to leave school without the skills that will be required of them in a globalized—and in some ways unforgiving—economy. They will pay an enduring price in terms of declining wages and declining opportunities.

A big concern is what happens to immigrants once they get here. A study I conducted with my wife, Carola Suárez-Orozco (also a faculty member at Harvard), in California almost a decade ago revealed that something strange happens to the attitudes of immigrant children. The longer they stay here, the more negative they become in their basic attitudes toward school. Third-generation kids are more likely to get kicked out of school and to have disciplinary problems than second-generation kids. And second-generation kids are more likely to exhibit such behaviors than first-generation students. By the third generation, there is a kind of explosion of problems. This suggests the need for a fundamental change in those communities and certainly in the schools that produce these kinds of outcomes.

This mirrors the epidemiological paradox found in the fact that length of residency in the U.S. is associated with increasing medical problems such as diabetes and obesity. Say you are a Mexican-born woman who moved to the state of California and gave birth to a baby. It is more likely that that baby, the baby of an immigrant, is going to be healthier than the baby of a Mexican-American woman who was born in Fresno County and never migrated, even though that second woman is doing much better in terms of socioeconomic standing. So even though immigrants tend to be poor, they also tend to be healthier than their nonimmigrant counterparts. (For more information, see the 1998 study, *From Generation to Generation: The Health and Well-Being of Immigrant Children*, issued by the National Research Council.)

What is fascinating about the study of immigration in the United States is that the U.S. is the only postmodern democracy in the world where immigration is both history and destiny. Immigration is at the very epicenter of our foundational narrative about how the country came to be the way it is. We love immigrants as they appear in a cultural narrative that is very pastoral, and the stories of the Irish immigration and the Italian immigration are great and celebrated. But today you can look at the editorial page of the *New York Times* from 1901 and just white out Irish, Italian, and Eastern European, and pencil in Mexican, Chinese, and Haitian. The structure of the narrative is almost uncannily identical, and it reflects the same kinds of concerns: they are not going to learn English, they are not going to adapt, therefore they are not going to make it. We know what happened with that wave of immigrants.

There is a history, of course, of compulsory monolingualism in the United States. The first and second world wars really made the U.S. a cemetery for languages, as one of my colleagues says. European immigrants brought their languages to the U.S., and these languages were asphyxiated over time—languages like German and Italian, which had initially thrived in this country. Will Spanish go the way of German and Japanese and Italian? Unfortunately, the debate around language tends to be narrow and somewhat offensive, dominated by ideologues. We don't really see how languages might add to the general cultural stock of the nation, yet in Switzerland most cab drivers speak several languages.

The question also has profound national security implications in the context of the aftermath of September 11. Recently in Boston we all went into a panic, expecting to be attacked, because one of our intelligence services mistranslated or got wrong some communication in Arabic, one of the major world languages. English is pushing aside other languages, and when languages die, ways of comprehending the world disappear with them. It is a paradox that, while English has become possibly the most hegemonic language in history, we panic about kids speaking Spanish or Fijian or Chinese.

Response from
Harold L. Hodgkinson

Harold Hodgkinson, director of the Center for Demographic Policy at the Institute for Educational Leadership in Washington, DC, argues that middle-class suburban communities are becoming more diverse, better reflecting the racial and ethnic makeup of the United States. As this happens, discussions about inequity, which until recently have focused on race, will shift to considerations of economic class.

How will we respond to the fact that more than 25 percent of today's children live below the poverty line? Furthermore, as the baby-boom generation gets older, will aging baby boomers have an interest in supporting the public schooling of "other people's kids" once their own children and grandchildren are grown? Or will their political power be used to divert resources elsewhere?

There has been a large increase recently in the number of middle-class blacks, most of whom live in the suburbs. Only 12 percent of the parents of black baby-boomers had a high school diploma, compared to 65 percent of all black parents today. Black high school graduation rates are now almost the same as for whites, and blacks are catching up in terms of completing some college. Getting blacks into college is no longer an issue, but getting them to complete college is. This raises a couple of policy questions.

How much of the difference in performance is based on "race"—"race" is in quotes because you can now identify yourself with as many races as you want on the new Census forms—and how much of that difference is based on wealth?

With 25 percent of black households having a higher income than the white average, it is clear that being black is no longer a universally handicapping factor. It is still terribly important and we can't overlook racial differences, but the only universally handicapping condition in education today is poverty. If you are born into poverty, your chances of success are much worse than if you are not. Whatever your skin color, if you are born poor, you are going to need somebody's assistance in order to maximize your potential.

Principals say the number-one cause of problems in their schools is low income. When you see the math scores on the National Educational Longitudinal Survey for Asians, whites, Hispanics, and blacks, much of the variance is based on wealth. Wealthy Asians do better than poor Asians, wealthy Hispanics do better than poor Hispanics, etc. Clearly, we need to find out how to increase the scores of poor kids.

So, while we may not be doing well on the TIMSS (Third International Mathematics and Science Study), we are number one in terms of childhood poverty. Nobody can touch us on that one. If we are going to compare our schools with those of other nations, it behooves us to have a look at the percentage of children in poverty. If you look at all the poor kids in the United States—14 million as of 1999—nine million are white. However, that's only 16 percent of the white population of kids. But while fewer than half as many blacks are poor (4.2 million), they make up 37 percent of the black population. The percentages are similar for Hispanic kids.

Now, combine these factors with other considerations, such as the age of the baby boomers. In 2025, one-fifth of the population will be older than 65. The baby-boom generation did not have enough babies to perpetuate itself, and for the first time there will be as many seniors as young people. And if we look ahead to 2040, which is not that far away, we're going to find a time in which we have more people over age 80 than we have preschool children. Not only will these seniors be out of school, but their kids will be out of school, and probably their grandchildren as well. Given these circumstances, it won't be at all surprising if many of those people are not kindly disposed toward paying taxes to support the public schools.

Response from
Robert J. Murphy

It may seem obvious that voters who don't have children or grandchildren in schools should still be concerned with public education. After all, education is an important means of reducing social inequities, a key to a healthier, safer, and more prosperous society for everyone. If that is true, should school leaders and teachers get more involved in the political battles that determine the quality of public schools as places to teach and learn? Robert J. Murphy, director of professional practice and government relations for the Connecticut Education Association, addresses this important question.

I've worked with schools in Waterbury and New London (Connecticut) that have a few common elements. They both have large bilingual populations, high poverty rates, and unbelievable mobility rates. One school in Waterbury reports a 120 percent mobility rate. When I asked the principal, "What is this all about?" she replied, "It's all about staying one step ahead of the landlord."

So teachers are saying, "I have the right to teach these kids, and they have the right to be taught. But I can't teach them if they're not there, or if they're there for a month and then they're gone, and then they come back a month later."

What causes this? One cause might be a welfare reform initiative that's passed, for political reasons, at the top of the food chain but that affects our ability to teach at the bottom of the food chain. Educators need to get involved in these kinds of issues. Yet in my business—the union business—we have been gun-shy in the last decade about confronting issues that we think the public might interpret as being social issues, when they think we ought to be focusing on student achievement.

I recently heard a story about a community that voted down an initiative to fluoridate the water. No one talked about the real value of fluoridation, though in many places it has helped a generation of children go to school with a lot better teeth. We should get involved in these issues. When I left Massachusetts, there were 180,000 kids younger than 18 who had no health insurance. Doesn't it impact a kid's ability to learn when she or he is not getting appropriate medical care? We need to roll up our sleeves and get involved in the nasty business of policymaking, of influencing political decisions that have an impact on our ability to do our work.

SUGGESTED QUESTIONS TO BEGIN DISCUSSION

1. What skills does a global economy require? Are there ways your school/district could do better at teaching and/or assessing those skills?

2. How would you explain Suárez-Orozco's finding that immigrant students get increasingly negative about schooling the longer they stay in the United States? Have you seen examples of this behavior in second- and third-generation immigrants in your school?

3. Hodgkinson suggests that class will replace race as the focus of social conflict and concern in the United States. How do you see this new focus in relationship to your school?

4. Why should voters who don't have children or grandchildren in schools be concerned with public education?

5. What proposed local or state policies will have an impact on your school—and can you and your staff affect the outcome? Why should you try?

4

Does More Choice Mean Less Equity?

Chester E. Finn, Jr.

See responses from Pedro A. Noguera (p. 50)
and Gary Orfield (p. 52)

*Charters schools have been around for just over a decade and
have had an unmistakable impact on the national education
debate. It's been much less clear how charters—schools
funded with public dollars but exempt from many of the requirements of traditional public schools—have affected student learning and educational opportunity in the communities in which they operate.*

*Do charters and other forms of choice increase opportu-
nity by offering parents and students more options? Or, as
some critics charge, do they exacerbate the inequities of the*

current system through de facto exclusion of the poor, the learning disabled, and other students who might be perceived as being more difficult to teach? Chester E. Finn, Jr., the John M. Olin Fellow at the Manhattan Institute and president of the Thomas B. Fordham Foundation, considers the place of charters in the school reform debate.

When it comes to education reform in the U.S. today, three big ideas are stalking the land. The first is the most familiar. I'm going to call it "more of the same": more money, more inputs, more services, more professional development, more technical assistance, and on and on. The assumption here is that our K–12 education system knows how to do better and wants to do better but lacks the necessary resources or expertise.

Hence, it is said by those who follow the strategy that better results will follow from—take your choice—smaller classes, more teachers, teachers and principals who spent more time in ed school, more technology, more special programs, more hours in the day, more days in the year, new books, different books, new computers, different computers, new software, different software, on down the list. This has long been the nation's chief approach to making schools better. It resembles our approach to making a lot of things better: install a larger engine, replace the tires, and add more chrome.

In pursuit of this strategy, per pupil spending in U.S. public schools has approximately tripled in real terms, that is, in constant dollars, since the 1950s—since I was in school.

That is not to say that every school has the money it needs, or that some states and communities don't face whopping deficits in their school budgets. It means only that we're spending a lot more money on K–12 education today than we did in the past.

The main problem with the "more-inputs" strategy is that it hasn't worked very well. At least it hasn't worked well nationally, not if by working we mean significantly boosting student achievement. U.S. scores remain essentially flat at an unacceptably low level of performance.

Because the more-inputs strategy has not worked well, most states have embarked on a second approach to primary and secondary education reform. Most people call it the standards movement, or the accountability movement, or standards-based reform. This is the reform strategy that underlies the federal education legislation, the No Child Left Behind Act. Indeed, it is the main event in most states today. You might say this approach to reform half trusts the system to do better. But it creates, from outside the system, and usually from higher levels of political authority such as the state, prescribed results that the system is told to produce. It then creates tests and other measures to determine how well those results are being produced and establishes various rewards and sanctions designed to prod the system into making changes in order to produce those results. It's a very behaviorist premise about what drives change: that if what we really care about are academic results, we need to focus directly on those results. And the way to do that is to specify the skills and knowledge kids ought to learn, install reliable measures of progress, and make people accountable for their results. That is to say, reward them when they achieve the desired results and intervene in some way when they don't.

How well is standards-based reform working? My view is so-so. A lot of states are setting poor standards. Many are administering misaligned or incomplete tests. Most of them haven't gotten very far in terms of consequences for success and failure, especially the kind of consequences that bear on grownups. States are a lot faster to make consequences fall on kids than on adults.

Meanwhile, to complicate matters further, a third education reform strategy has landed in our midst. This one doesn't believe in centralized, top-down reform. It believes instead in grassroots-, marketplace-, and competition-style change. For simplicity, it's often called the choice movement, though it takes many forms. It includes charter schools, outsourced or contract schools, all sorts of voucher and scholarship and open enrollment plans, and a number of other ways to foster diversity and competition in K–12 education.

The theory behind choice-based reform holds that the regular system is most likely to reform in response to pressure arising from competition; that is, from loss of market share, as they say in the business world. The theory also holds that, while we're waiting for the school system to get its act together, choice policies help the kids who benefit directly from them—that is, those who get to change their own education circumstances with the aid of charter schools, vouchers, or whatever. These are typically poor and disadvantaged kids.

The average charter school in the United States is only about two years old. Which means, incidentally, that it is hard to draw any final conclusions about how they're working. It also means from a parent's standpoint that when they enroll their kid in such a school they are taking a risk. They are gambling on a school with no track record. They are not only gambling on a school with no track record, they are often gambling on a school that is in a makeshift facility and poorly funded, because the average charter school has about 80 percent of the annual per pupil operating revenues of the average regular public school.

How desperate do you have to be to take that gamble with your own kid? To entrust your kid to a brand new school with no track record in a makeshift facility that is lacking some of the elements that a lot of people would think of as pretty basic elements of a school? How desperate do you have to be, and what does that say about the schools they're leaving behind and the experience their kids are having in them?

Here are nine reasons why charter schools hold promise for reforming public schooling in the United States:

1. There is plenty of demand, both to start schools and to enroll kids in them. Many states are bumping up against their legislatively mandated caps on how many of these schools are allowed. Most charter schools have waiting lists. The country could easily absorb thousands more charter schools and hundreds of thousands more places in them for kids.

2. On the whole, customer satisfaction is high. That's not to say everybody likes everything about his or her charter school, only that most people view their charter schools as a big improvement over what they had before.

3. Charter schools are fomenting innovation on a number of fronts. Some of them, frankly, are innovating more than they need to. They are reinventing wheels that were already out there waiting to be spun. Many, though, are pioneering fresh organizational models, imaginative curricula, remarkable uses of technology, and unconventional ways of responding to kids with special needs, distinctive ways of recovering dropouts, and so on.

4. There are some terrific charter schools out there in which I would happily enroll any child I cared about. This is not to say we don't have some terrific schools in the regular public and private sectors. We certainly do. My own impression is that if I dropped down out of the sky into a random school, the odds of my thinking well of it or liking what I saw there would be somewhat higher if it were a random charter school than if it were a random traditional public school, or possibly even a random traditional private school.

5. Charters are turning out to be compatible with other important education reforms that are under way simultaneously in the United States. They turn out to be compatible with the standards movement and its approach to accountability. They turn out to be compatible with school privatization and outsourcing efforts. They turn out to be compatible with interesting developments on the technology front. And some of them are turning out to be compatible in interesting ways with home-schooling.

6. Politically, their appeal has been bipartisan. We've seen that in Congress as well as in many states. Republicans

tend to like them because they crack the monopoly and empower parents. Democrats tend to like them because they retain public accountability and are disproportionately serving poor and minority kids. Conservatives view them as a welcome form of school choice. Liberals see them as a way of reinventing government and reforming public education.

7. Charters turn out to be a solution to an astonishing array of different problems. I've been struck by how charters and virtual charters, of which we have about 15 operating in the United States today, make it possible for home-schoolers to base their instruction on an organized curriculum; by how a few imaginative districts are using the charter law to circumvent their own bureaucracies and teacher union contracts, deploying school personnel or meeting school needs in ways they couldn't do under their own usual rules and procedures. I'm struck, too, by how many different kinds of communities have been able to use the charter mechanism to create schools that meet their own needs or express their own values.

8. The charter movement is bringing all sorts of interesting people into education and keeping them there. These include people who I think would not be involved at all if it weren't for this opportunity. And it's bringing resources into education, particularly private capital invested in charter schools by some of the many entrepreneurs who are drawn in to operate schools and serve schools using the charter mechanism.

9. Charters are helping people glimpse a different kind of education future. Instead of viewing charters as excep-

tions on the margins, as some sort of pressure-release valve for some of the pent-up steam in the boiler, we're beginning to read about places that are at least considering chartering every single school in the community. We're reading and hearing about charter districts, about virtual charter schools serving people wherever they happen to be. Maybe ten years after their beginnings, charters are now becoming a preview of tomorrow's central educational design.

According to Finn, although they do hold promise, charters are nevertheless plagued by problems. They include 1) a lack of leadership in business and government to support the charter movement; 2) "bad apples" to which critics can point for evidence of the failure of charters; 3) the difficulty of starting and maintaining a charter school; 4) authorizers or sponsors, such as boards of education, that do not always support charters effectively; 5) the presence of active political opponents; 6) the need for school officials to become more adept at managing the accountability challenges they face; and 7) the "mixed signals" that charters have sent so far in terms of academic achievement.

A SNAPSHOT OF CHARTER SCHOOLS
(ESTIMATES)

Number of charter schools in the U.S.: 2,400

Number of students enrolled: 600,000

Average age (in years) of a U.S. charter school: 2

Percentage of Michigan students enrolled in charter schools: 4

Percentage of Arizona students enrolled in charter schools: 8

Some U.S. cities in which more than 15 percent of students attend charter schools:

Dayton, OH

Kansas City, MO

Washington, DC

Response from
Pedro A. Noguera

Pedro A. Noguera, the Judith K. Dimon Professor of Communities and Schools at the Harvard Graduate School of Education and a specialist in urban education issues, cites three elements common to charter schools that he believes are well worth replicating: a strong mission, a commitment to accountability, and a sense of community. But Noguera also sees the dangers in treating charter schools as a solution to a complex set of educational problems.

My main interest is in how we make good schools available to kids, and not in defending a system. That's the reason I generally support charters. Having said that, I want to caution us from making sweeping generalizations about charters, as I believe Chester Finn did. I've seen more than just a few bad apples out there. I see lots of charters that are struggling. I remember that when Jerry Brown was elected mayor of Oakland he wanted to create charters throughout the whole city. I encouraged him to look first at the charters he had, because they were all very bad schools.

I was involved in a study led by Amy Stewart Wells at UCLA in which we looked at 45 charter schools in the state of California. Several of those schools were struggling, but at the same time, several of them were great schools that offered good alternatives for kids. There are a few concerns, though, that I think we need to be aware of.

One is that charters tend to have much higher turnover, among both leaders and teachers, than regular schools. I think some of this has to do with the extra demands that are placed on teachers in charters, and I think there's good reason to be concerned about that with respect to continuity and stability.

I think, second, that almost every charter I've run across has a major problem with facilities. That is, there's been no provision in most states to provide adequate facilities for charters. So in many cases, charters are in poor facilities. I know of one case where kids had no access to bathrooms at their charter school. This is a problem that many states have not addressed.

Third, many charters are subject to the same kind of political infighting that we see in large districts, just at a smaller level. That is, in many districts there are huge conflicts between the principal or school leader and the board, or between parents and teachers. This is in part because they have not thought through how to work out a division of labor and an understanding of what the roles are. And so we see many charters that have, in fact, been destroyed by this political infighting.

Finally, there's a lot of evidence to show that charters are more segregated than regular schools and that many charters actually screen out troubled kids and kids who have special needs. I think there are good reasons to be concerned about who has been excluded from charters. We need to make sure that all kids have access to a good education, not just those who are lucky enough to be picked to go to a charter.

Response from Gary Orfield

Concerns about unequal access are among the most common objections to the way charters and other choice-based reforms play out in practice. Gary Orfield, professor of education and social policy at Harvard University, notes that school choice has been used in the past as a strategy to keep schools segregated by race. He says that current choice initiatives can have a similar effect unless measures are taken to ensure equity.

I would like to offer a little different perspective on the origin and significance of our experience with choice. Basically, choice arose as a serious dimension of U.S. education out of the desegregation experience. It was not significant until then. It arose primarily in the South in the 1960s as a way to avoid desegregation and was called "freedom of choice." And it did avoid it effectively, since about 98 percent of black students ended up in totally segregated schools ten years after the *Brown* decision. Under freedom of choice, no whites ever chose to go into black schools. I don't know of any place in thousands of districts where this occurred.

Choice then took a different form in the middle 1970s, after the U.S. Supreme Court blocked access to suburban schools for desegregation purposes. Cities that had to desegregate then tried to do it through choice and magnets and tried to create something that would be attractive to families of all racial groups. Cincinnati and Milwaukee pioneered this on a large scale. They had some significant success, and hundreds of schools around the country were created by court orders under the federal magnet school program. There's evidence that these magnet schools do a better job than regular public schools.

What we found is that until you add certain elements to choice, choices are very stratifying. If you just have first-come, first-served and you don't have good information, you don't have good transportation, and so forth, the advantaged families get there first and they get the best choices. This makes the schools even more unequal. Successful desegregation plans have transportation, good information, desegregation standards, parent outreach and information systems, and so forth.

Now, what we have under charter schools are magnet schools without any of the civil rights protections. They don't usually provide transportation, they don't offer good information, and they don't have desegregation standards. They often don't provide for handicapped and language-minority children. I think that choice is a powerful tool if it is added to real educational options and if it is made available fairly. Ironically, those who are pushing for vouchers and charters don't favor expanding the forms of choice that have proven successful, such as magnet schools and interdistrict choice. Both forms are available in St. Louis, for example, where 14,000 black children go to suburban schools and have twice as high a graduation rate as their nonparticipating peers.

There's a program in Milwaukee in which several thousand kids go to suburban schools by choice, and that program is opposed by the same conservative forces that are pushing for expansion of voucher programs. What we ought to do first is expand choice with good equity provisions inside public schools, support good-quality magnets, and introduce the choice of suburban schools for kids who are in isolated and inferior schools. And we should try to create regional magnets that can serve entire metropolitan areas, and make those good schools available to everyone.

SUGGESTED QUESTIONS TO BEGIN DISCUSSION

1. Consider the three approaches to school reform cited by Finn: the "more-inputs" approach, the standards/account-ability approach, and the marketplace approach. Which of these approaches do you think drives most of the reform decisions in your school or district? In your state? Do you think the decisions made under this approach are effective? What approach best reflects your personal philosophy about education reform?

2. Which of the nine factors that Finn cites as strengths of charter schools do you find to be compelling reasons why this "experiment" should continue?

3. Noguera states that he is interested more in improving schools than in "defending a system." Can schools ever be reformed effectively through changes in structures or systems?

4. Orfield says that in order to ensure equity, school choice plans require "transportation, good information, desegregation standards, parent outreach and information systems." Do you agree? If so, what might some of the plans to implement these factors look like?

5

Closing the
Achievement Gap

Belinda Williams

Belinda Williams is a cognitive psychologist who has studied the achievement patterns of culturally diverse and socioeconomically disadvantaged students for more than 25 years. The editor of Closing the Achievement Gap: A Vision for Changing Beliefs and Practices *(published by the Association for Supervision and Curriculum Development), Williams shares her concern that the recent efforts to raise academic achievement through accountability initiatives have done little to address the gaps in achievement among groups of students.*

Most people would look at the graphic shown here as Figure 1 and feel somewhat comforted by the notion that achievement is improving for all children, those in both high-poverty and low-poverty schools. One could conclude that all we need to do is figure out what we're doing right and continue doing that.

However, if you focus on what's being indicated by the vertical arrow, this points out a tremendous challenge, what I call the *real* challenge for this country in the 21st century. The arrow alerts us to the reality that we could successfully improve achievement for all children and at the same time actively contribute to the development of a permanent underclass of people. As long as there are gaps in achievement between groups of students, we are not doing all that we need to do to make sure that all children are going to be competitive in the 21st century.

This is the central issue that I have studied for nearly 30 years. Unlike a lot of researchers who have looked at issues of achievement and ways to improve it, my initial question was, "Why are there gaps in achievement among groups of children?" I have not focused my attention on the gaps between any particular groups. I have looked at gaps in achievement among a number of populations rather than tried to explain the gaps between blacks and whites or between advantaged and disadvantaged students. I have looked for other gaps because, until and unless we're able to explain the gaps that exist among a number of groups, we will not successfully understand the gaps that exist between any groups.

I took this data from a federal evaluation of Title I that was disseminated in a study a couple of years ago. When I an-

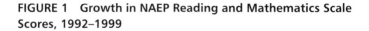

FIGURE 1 Growth in NAEP Reading and Mathematics Scale Scores, 1992–1999

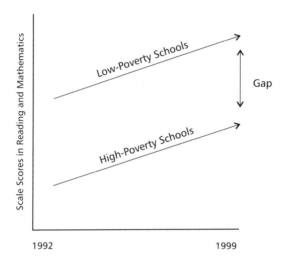

alyzed this data (see Figures 2 and 3), I came away confused and troubled. In this report the overarching conclusion was that the introduction of standards could make a difference in achievement patterns.

When I looked at it, though, I thought, "What are they basing that on?" If you examine the data, there are at least two alarming facts represented. One is that, if you look at the reading scale scores of nine-year-olds in 1988, you see that the average for students in high-poverty schools was 190. And if you look at the average for these students in 1996, you see that it was 188. So where is the evidence that the introduction of standards has made a difference? The conclusion

FIGURE 2   Trends in NAEP Reading Performance

Average scale scores of nine-year-old public school students, by poverty level of school (1988–1996)

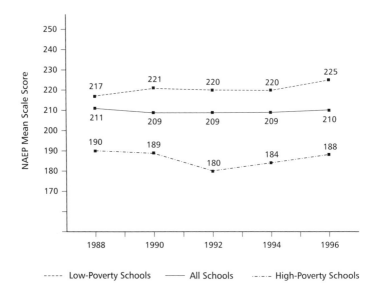

----- Low-Poverty Schools   ——— All Schools   ·—·—· High-Poverty Schools

Highest-poverty school = 76% to 100% of students eligible for free or reduced-price lunch. Low-poverty school = 0% to 25% of students eligible for free or re-duced-price lunch. Scale scores are 0–500.

Source: U.S. Department of Education, National Center for Education Statistics, National Assessment of Educational Progress, NAEP Reading Trends, unpublished tabulations, 1998.

FIGURE 3   Trends in NAEP Mathematics Performance

Average scale scores of nine-year-old public school students, by poverty level of school (1988–1996)

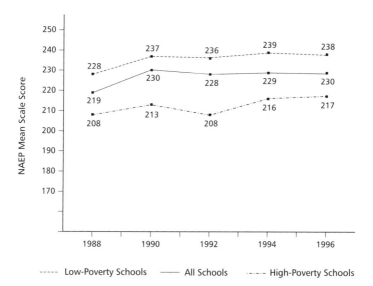

Highest-poverty school = 76% to 100% of students eligible for free or reduced-price lunch. Low-poverty school = 0% to 25% of students eligible for re-duced-price lunch. Scale scores are 0–500.

Source: U.S. Department of Education, National Center for Education Statistics, National Assessment of Educational Progress, NAEP Mathematics Trends, un-published tabulations, 1998.

was based on the fact that standards were introduced in 1992 with the reauthorization of Title I. And, as you can observe, between 1992 and 1996 there was some improvement.

But if you compare the reading scale score points of 1996 and 1988, you observe that there was no improvement. In fact, there was a slight decline in the average scale score points in reading. Also, if you subtract the average scale score points between high-poverty and low-poverty schools, you can see that the difference in 1988 was 27 scale score points, and in 1996 the gap was 37 scale score points. So where is the evidence that the introduction of standards made the difference in achievement?

My initial assumption was that I had obviously misunderstood something, that the federal government could not have released a report with a major conclusion that was not supported by its own data. And yet, if you examine a copy of that report, you will see that the overarching recommendation from this data was that we needed to continue to introduce standards across the country. As I'm sure you are aware, every state in this country is following that mandate, with the exception of Iowa, which has decided not to emphasize the development or introduction of standards.

So I looked at the list of prestigious educators who had reviewed this document, and I began to call them. Of course, today when you call people, you seldom talk to a real person. You typically get a voice message, and that is what happened. But I left my question, my name, and my phone on a number of voice mails. No one returned my call. So I started going down the list to call again. I reached only one person who had reviewed this document. When I posed my question, he said,

"No, you have not misinterpreted the data. Your interpretations, questions, and concerns are accurate."

So I asked, "Then how did the government disseminate a report that was so misleading to the rest of the country?" His response was that they didn't know what else to do, because they didn't understand the data. Since the information could be instrumental in the reauthorization of Title I—and they were concerned about losing that $8 billion a year—they tried to draw as many conclusions as possible.

We are experiencing the implications of that report's recommendation, which is a major emphasis on standards across the country. What I have concluded does not suggest that we don't need standards, but I think we have to reposition the interpretation and understanding of what standards can and cannot do. If we continue to simplify our focus and prioritize standards, then, as this data suggests, we might show some improvement in achievement, but we might also witness an increase in the gaps in achievement between groups of children.

Before I go any further, I want to clarify the nature of the achievement gap. I've been discussing this issue for 25 or 30 years, and I've come to understand that not everybody is clear about what the gap is and is not. When you analyze bell curves, and I simply use bell curves for the sake of making this distinction, you see that within every group, within every population, there is a distribution of achievement patterns (see Figure 4). In every population, there are individuals who achieve at one end of the continuum and individuals who achieve at the other end. I emphasize this point because in the overall society—and we have some evidence that this per-

FIGURE 4   Individual Differences vs. Group Differences

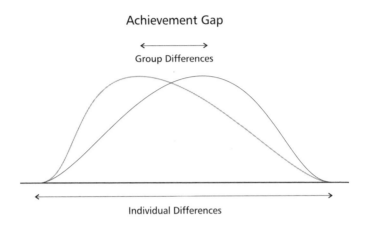

ception and understanding exist in our public schools—there is an assumption that, because there are group differences in achievement, every individual in one group is less able or capable than every individual in another group.

We need to be clear that that is not the case, that in every population there are individuals who achieve at one end of the continuum or the other. This is not an argument against the need for remedial programs, special education, or both. My emphasis is on understanding that we're talking about group differences, and this notion has implications for that slogan that you hear people use all the time, and that I often see posted when I enter schools: "All children can learn." We have to understand that in every population, within every group, there are some children who will be exceptionally challenged to learn at the same level as other children. Therefore, the goal must be to make sure that every individual in every group who is capable of learning at high levels has that opportunity. Until we focus on and make those distinctions, then we will continue to misinterpret and misunderstand those dynamics that are contributing to group differences.

We have an achievement gap between groups of children, and those bell curves could represent group achievement patterns that exist between various cultural groups or various socioeconomic groups or racial groups. They are not limited to any particular group comparison.

We are clear about what politicians have decided is the issue: testing and more testing. But one of the key elements of any conversation about reform must be a discussion about what we know about how learning occurs. I find it fascinating that when groups of educators come together, they're not necessarily talking about the available knowledge about how learning occurs. That, I would suggest, is the conversation that is going to help us give true meaning to the slogan, "All *groups of* children can learn."

We have structures in public schools across the country that enable educators to make decisions about children almost as soon as they enter school. We have a system of testing that contributes to the placement of children in various programs or tracks. When you look at disaggregated data in most schools across the country, what is obvious and clear is that we have disproportionate numbers of socioeconomically disadvantaged children, children in high-poverty situations, and children of color who are overrepresented in programs or tracks for students classified as "special needs," "at-risk," "impaired," "underachieving," "culturally deprived," "problem," and "slow"—as well as "failure." Those same groups of children are *under*represented in programs or tracks for "gifted," "talented," "college-bound," "level-one," and "honors" students.

Until we revisit the system of education in this country and think about how we're making decisions about children—and what impact those decisions have on the nature of the learning experience in public schools—then we're not likely to see much difference in the gaps in achievement between groups of children.

SUGGESTED QUESTIONS TO BEGIN DISCUSSION

1. Do achievement gaps exist in your school or district? If so, between what groups? To what do you attribute these gaps?

2. What strategies might you implement to address the achievement gaps that exist in your school or district?

3. What connections, if any, do you see between the tracking that Williams discusses and the achievement gap? How do you think tracking and detracking affect gaps among groups of students?

4. Williams expresses concern that, although some test scores are rising, gaps between groups of students remain. Should school reform efforts be revised if such developments result, or is raising the level of all students in itself a worthy goal?

6

Using Afterschool Programs to Raise Achievement

Gil G. Noam

*Gil G. Noam, director of the Program in Afterschool Educa-
tion and Research (PAER) and associate professor of education
at the Harvard Graduate School of Education, believes that
strong afterschool programs are needed to fill what he calls an
"open space that is very, very long for kids." Noam says these
programs not only can provide children with productive ways
to spend their free time, but also can support achievement
during the school day in a variety of ways.*

think virtually all educators share the strong sense that we're putting too much emphasis and too much of a burden on schools. They are supposed to handle everything: mental health issues, social work issues, community problems, and violence. All of these issues are now placed on the schools, and they're connected to achievement.

If children are abused, or their parents divorce, or they have lots of problems, then they are just not going to approach education in the way we would hope. With this in mind, I see two different areas as being linked. One is out-of-school time and the organization of afterschool time. The other is mental health support in many of its forms. I believe these two issues belong together, and that if we use funds well and are thoughtful about it, we actually have a big chance to make a difference. But I also think there's a danger that the funds will be used in ways that are ultimately *not* going to help children, especially inner-city children, do well and reduce the achievement gap.

Most school administrators are aware of how many hours kids are in school and how many hours they are out of school. Yet, even though we know all this, we have not really organized socially and societally this open space that is very, very long for kids.

There are three trends that have come together to make this a significant issue. The first trend has to do with employment patterns and welfare reform. The afterschool movement began at a time when the Clinton administration began to reform welfare. Suddenly women, especially poor women, were asked to work. Once they were asked to work it was very important to figure out what to do with the kids while their mothers were working. If you look at the increase in the work force over the last 20 years, especially among women, you see that more than 75 percent of children come from single-parent homes or homes where both parents work.

The second trend has to do with an emphasis on crime prevention. Most policemen will agree that afterschool time is critical, because that is the time when many crimes occur.

The third trend is school reform. It is clear that if you want to increase children's academic achievement, you have to organize their afterschool time. You have to figure out who is going to do homework with them. Who is actually going to make them focus on academic issues? The school day is too short for this work to be accomplished there.

We need to work together to integrate our out-of-school initiatives. There are currently two main movements in out-of-school time: the youth development movement and the school reform movement. These efforts are really about having an integrated focus on how schools, communities, the arts, museums, and other institutions work together in a new, collaborative way. We need to bring the creativity of institutions like the New England Aquarium and the Museum of Science together with the schools, the communities, the YMCA, and the Boys and Girls Clubs. And that is actually happening. While there was a lot of struggle in the beginning of this integrated focus, I think we're now at a point where all of these organizations and institutions are beginning to address how we make these afterschool hours academically useful.

I think this is a tremendous chance, and I think we have a great chance to blow it. Why? Because afterschool programs will only be supported in their present form if we can show academic outcomes. It is not enough that parents know that their kids are safe. It's not enough that the crime rate is going down, even though these things are important. This kind of innovation, this attempt to reorganize children's and youths' out-of-school time, is only going to work if we can also show that it makes a difference academically.

A good program is typically seen as one that has both academic and non-academic components. Such a program is often either in a school or in the community. One hour is spent on homework and homework support. How much time we spend on homework becomes a class issue, because in order for kids to succeed it is important that some adults are there to help them with homework. Everyone expects this. The sixth grader, the seventh grader, the eighth grader needs support from some adult other than a teacher to do his or her homework. And if you consider immigrants who don't speak the language, it becomes an issue of promoting democracy to provide environments in which kids can actually be supported in doing their homework. Some people are thinking carefully about how homework help can be offered in a child-centered, supportive, and creative way, building on the concept that afterschool programs should have small learning centers within them.

The second hour after school is typically spent on sports and other activities. This is the development component with the YMCA and the Boys and Girls Clubs that gives kids fun time beyond academic work. The third hour is typically spent on project-based learning. This might involve service learning or other forms of learning. Of course, the hope is that you can use the afterschool program as a kind of experiment to develop programs that in turn will penetrate the school in different ways.

The reason I'm concerned about these programs is that, like many other programs, they get evaluated. We are working under the notion that evaluation is very important, and I agree with that. But what is happening is that before programs can become strong, they generally start out weak. Think of how long we've had to build up schools and how short a span of time we've had to build up good out-of-school programs, to figure out how to link them to the school day and make them relevant. The federal government is giving one evaluation organization a $12 million grant to evaluate afterschool programs, and I think we're going to have an evaluation that won't show a tremendous amount of positive results because we haven't built up the programs enough to show strong results. Rather than having evaluations built in so that we can use them to strengthen the system over time, we often use evaluations as a kind of early indicator of success or failure, and then we make decisions about future funding based on evaluations that are done too early.

When we look at carefully designed studies we see the beginnings of promising results, good programs that focus on academics in the ways that I mentioned, either directly through homework or through projects. These well-run programs show that kids do better academically through participation in afterschool programs.

I don't think resiliency by itself or fun by itself is sufficient. Our goals should be and will continue to be the academic achievement of kids. Kids feel better when they achieve. The course of their lives is much better. We know this from studies. I think we should use afterschool funding in a productive way without being over-controlling. We should allow creativity with clear standards, and the standards don't have to involve just testing. Then I think we will have used these afterschool funds at this moment in history—and it really is a significant moment—in a productive way.

SUGGESTED QUESTIONS TO BEGIN DISCUSSION

1. Do you agree with Noam's suggestion that society expects a great deal from schools beyond academic achievement? In your opinion, are schools bearing too much of a burden for societal problems that affect children?

2. Do you believe afterschool programs should be closely connected to homework and the school day or have other goals? How much emphasis should be placed on academic achievement? Why?

3. Noam suggests that many afterschool programs are evaluated too early, before they have had a chance to demonstrate success. Have you had such an experience with a premature evaluation of a program in your school or district? How did it affect the program?

4. What kinds of evaluation standards do you think should be applied to afterschool programs? What kind of standards do you think are inappropriate? Why?

7

Learning to Challenge Assumptions

Richard Rothstein

See responses from Richard F. Elmore (p. 84)
and Nat LaCour (p. 87)

School leaders, policymakers, administrators, and other
stakeholders need to be skeptical of conventional wisdom
about policy problems and proposed solutions. Too often we
charge into new reform efforts believing we have a complete
understanding of what the problem is, which is not always
the case, warns New York Times *columnist Richard Roth-*
stein. In fact, Rothstein says that policymakers and adminis-
trators often make big decisions based on faulty assump-
tions—errors that may take years to correct.

There is a widespread assumption that we're going to face an enormous teacher shortage over the next few years and that this will affect how we approach professional development and the kinds of people that we hire in education. I think few people in education are actually thinking carefully about this issue. I suspect there's not going to be a teacher shortage but rather a big teacher surplus.

Look at what's going on in the economy with the collapse of the dot-coms and economic growth that is certainly going to be slower than what we had in the 1990s. When young people at the end of their sophomore year in college decide what to major in and whether to enter into a teacher education program, teaching is going to look a lot more attractive today than it did two and three years ago. In a few years, you're going to begin to see that reflected in the kinds of applicants you get for teaching positions.

Now, I may be wrong about this. Nobody has a crystal ball that can predict the future. The best economic analysts in the country don't know. But it's at least an issue that administrators ought to be considering, rather than simply accepting the assumption that's widely repeated about the teacher shortage. It affects what they do about salary plans for their teaching force; it affects what kinds of people they hire, what kinds of professional development they plan, and what kinds of relationships they have with colleges of education.

Here's another assumption. For 20 years we've been in the midst of an intensive school reform drive. It began—and continues today—on the assumption that the economy of the 21st century is technologically very advanced and requires a much higher skill level than the economy of the past. We hear claims that the number of jobs requiring a college education is going to grow enormously and that the skill base of the economy is expanding. In fact, none of it's true.

It's time for educators to begin to think more skeptically about these kinds of claims and about their implications. The report "A Nation at Risk," which came out in 1983, said that the United States was engaged in unilateral disarmament because of the failures of our education system. We were going to lose an economic war of competition with Japan and Western Europe. At the time we faced trade deficits with both, and virtually every analyst drew the conclusion that the trade deficit was the result of the failure of our schools to prepare productive workers. We were, the report said, losing a productivity race with other industrialized nations, such as Japan and Germany.

Twenty years later we've left the economies of Japan and Western Europe in the dust. The trade deficit still exists, but nobody thinks this reflects the inability of our economy to compete. We clearly out-compete every industrial power in the world. Yet where is the reflection about what this means for the education system? I'm not asking that anybody credit the education system for the relative economic success that the United States has enjoyed in the last ten years, but clearly it was wrong to blame the schools for the trade deficit and the economic problems that we had in the 1980s and early 1990s.

If it was wrong to blame the schools for that, then let's look at the kinds of reforms we're implementing and see whether they may be based on false premises. I'm not suggesting that the reforms are bad; maybe they're good reforms done for the wrong reasons. But if they're good reforms done for the wrong reasons, then there's a big danger that they might not be the right reforms.

Let me give one example. One consequence of this flawed economic theory is that we have accepted the idea that all students should learn algebra by eighth grade because algebra is the gatekeeper to calculus and everybody needs calculus to go to college. Even if they don't need to go to college, they need to use advanced mathematical skills in the workplace.

Technology in the modern economy is not increasing the skill level of the work force as a whole. In fact, when you do an analysis as we've done at the Economic Policy Institute of the skills required in the modern economy, what you find is that the average educational level needed in the work force in 1955 was only one-half of a school grade lower than the average educational requirement of jobs in 1995. That's how much the skill level had risen in an advanced technological economy.

This is not something you need to be a fancy economic analyst to perceive. If you look around you, you see that technology reduces the number of skills required for a particular job as much as it increases the skills required. To take the simplest example, a store clerk with a barcode scanner requires fewer arithmetic skills today than a store clerk needed 50 years ago when he or she had to add up a bill and add the sales tax, even if they used a calculator.

Of course there are some jobs where the requirements have increased, but on average they've not done so. The notion that everybody needs algebra because it's a gatekeeper to the economy is simply wrong. We have emphasized algebra to the exclusion of other mathematical skills that are more useful for some students. It's true that some students need advanced algebra or calculus, yet a citizen in this society needs a much more sophisticated understanding of probability and statistics than we're giving our students. We've made a choice about what to teach based on a flawed economic analysis that says that the kinds of technologically advanced occupations that require algebra and calculus are going to be uniform throughout the economy.

Let me address one other dangerous contextual myth that needs to be thought about more carefully: that we should hold all students to the same standards—that we "make no excuses." Clearly, many teachers and school administrators have had low expectations, too low, for children who came to school with disadvantages that middle-class children from professional homes did not have. However, the notion that we should hold the same expectations for all students is to ignore everything we know about the sociology of learning and about the way social class functions in this society. Students' academic achievement is not just the product of what students learn in schools or in their families. It is the product of a number of different circumstances and institutions, of the kinds of opportunities they have in their communities, of the culture that they come from.

There was a wonderful study done about ten years ago by Betty Hart and Todd R. Risley, two researchers at the University of Kansas. They went into homes and counted the number of words the children heard. The study was entitled, "Meaningful Differences in the Everyday Experience of Young American Children." The study basically found that children between the ages of six months and three years whose parents were college educated heard about 2,000 words an hour spoken in their environment. Children from working-class homes heard approximately 1,000 words an hour. And children from families on welfare heard something like 500 words an hour. Those children come to school with vastly different verbal ability. The challenge, of course, is to try to narrow the gap. But to think we can ignore the gap in the name of "making no excuses" is absurd. It's a way of avoiding our responsibility as educators to set realistic goals and then try to achieve them.

To give another example, we know that in some urban schools students have phenomenally high mobility rates. Clearly that affects learning. It's one of the big reasons for low achievement on the part of many low-income kids in urban settings. And a big reason for this mobility is that we have a housing crisis in this society. If I were a policymaker and wanted to raise the achievement of those students, I would expand the Section 8 housing program, because the reason the children are so mobile is that their parents are often moving to keep one step ahead of the rent. As a principal you can't create housing, but you can certainly do something to be a voice for student achievement.

A year and a half ago, the U.S. surgeon general issued a report in which he found that one-third of all poor children in this country had untreated dental cavities. Not all cavities result in toothaches, but let's assume that half of them do— that still affects one-sixth of all poor children. If we really want to narrow the achievement gap, we could start by making sure that one-sixth of the poor children in a school system don't have to sit through school with a toothache. We could do more to improve the test scores of low-income children by putting dental clinics in low-income schools than we could with higher standards, teacher training, and phonics.

It's a very simple reform. Yet because we "make no excuses" for low achievement, we prevent ourselves from looking at the systemic causes of that low achievement. By focusing only on things we can do in schools, we are guaranteeing failure. There's no way we're going to eliminate the academic gap by focusing only on schools and ignoring a much broader systemic view of how learning takes place.

Response from
Richard F. Elmore

Richard F. Elmore, the Gregory R. Anrig Professor of Educational Leadership at the Harvard Graduate School of Education, generally agrees with Rothstein. However, he also challenges school leaders to examine their own in-house operations more carefully, to ask questions about how things have always been done, and to challenge the assumptions that can mire schools in predictable patterns that serve no one well.

A message I get from Richard Rothstein is the need for a system of organizational response that is sensitive to the school environment, that engages in a lot of thoughtful focus and adaptation. Some systems are trying to build up the capacity at the school level to be focused and active, to face problems and to be agile enough in their internal processes to respond to the kinds of shifts that Richard talks about. Let me make this observation: the main claim to fame of the elementary and secondary education sector in our society is its failure to adapt to virtually every major systemic change in society over the last 100 years. So we have a fundamental pathology here.

I would predict that public policymakers are going to develop an increasingly skeptical attitude toward this sector's capacity to solve any problem we give it, and to look increasingly to simply bypass the sector, break it up, and move public money into private hands to provide services of all kinds. Much of the revenue currently financing the established bureaucratic structure in K–12 education is going to be spent on fee-for-service activities. That's what's happening in the rest of the economy, and the impatience with this institutional structure is really mounting on the part of policymakers. So the stakes are relatively high. Where is the voice of the professional educator on some of these issues?

On the expectation question, I think [Rothstein] is making a very good point. Granted, we may have a really crude theory at the moment about expectations and performance, but just look at the data. The data say that we have huge variability in quality of instruction and student performance, much larger than you can explain just by the social background of students. If you look at the TIMSS (Third International Mathematics and Science Study) research, we had the largest variations in measures of student performance and measures of quality of instruction among all the industrialized countries.

That points to a huge quality-control problem in our schools, and not just the low-performing ones. I don't want to be seen as arguing against systemic approaches or against being more active in the policy arena. But we need to take care of business in the schools first.

One of the things they discovered in District 2 in New York City—and this is very contextual, because it depends a lot on the demography and the geography of the community you're working in—is that once they started high-level instructional improvement in literacy and mathematics in their schools, mobility rates went down substantially. The reason is that, even though parents were moving at about the same rate they were before, they had a stronger incentive to keep their kids in the same schools because the kids were being treated well.

The district accepted that premise and then looked for ways to stabilize school enrollment for parents and students who were mobile. They discovered that just by modestly changing their transportation and school assignment rules they could take mobility down another notch. Now District 2 has schools with the highest proportions of low-income kids, but with mobility rates that are a tiny fraction of those of schools with similar social composition in the rest of New York City.

So yes, we should work on Section 8. We should work on health care and we should take a systemic view. But we also need to make sure that we're managing the core functions of the enterprise consistently with our theories about child development and learning so that when we lay the systemic stuff over the top, it has the intended effect.

Response from
Nat LaCour

Although he acknowledges the fact that many inner-city children are poorly served by their schools, Nat LaCour, executive vice president of the American Federation of Teachers (AFT), says it's also important to recognize the many success stories and build upon them. LaCour has been actively involved in leading the AFT's efforts to assist inner-city schools in raising students' academic achievement. He began his career as a biology teacher in the New Orleans public schools.

There are those who argue that our schools are failing. They maintain that little or no progress is taking place in our inner-city schools. This is not true. In Cleveland, educators are reaching out to families and businesses to lay the foundation for early reading skills. The CEO of the Cleveland Public Schools has been working with the Cleveland teacher union to improve professional development and to use research-backed practices in reading. The results might surprise those who are making a living thrashing public schools. Since 1998, fourth-grade reading scores in Cleveland have risen 44 percent.

In Corpus Christi, Texas, teachers help create the standards and adjust their grading policies to reflect the new goals. Students who struggle get extra help, but if they don't meet the standards, they don't get promoted to the next grade. The result? Scores for economically disadvantaged students have risen nearly 30 percent on the statewide tests since 1994. Corpus Christi is now the second highest performing urban school district in Texas. So there is in fact a lot of good news coming out of inner-city schools.

SUGGESTED QUESTIONS TO BEGIN DISCUSSION

1. Rothstein says that technology reduces the number of skills required for a particular job as much as it increases the skills required. The same could be said of technology's impact on classroom learning. How has technology changed the content and methods of learning in your school?

2. If academic achievement is more than the product of what students learn at school, as Rothstein argues, then what circumstances or institutions have positive and negative effects on how your students learn? What would you like to see changed?

3. Do you agree with Rothstein that slogans like "make no excuses" and "every child can learn" are misleading and harmful? Why? How has your school/district used these or similar slogans, and what have been the results in relationship to your students' learning?

4. Elmore suggests that the traditionally bureaucratic structure of K–12 education will be broken up, with private companies providing more and more services to schools. What are the plusses and minuses of privatization? Should privatization be limited?

5. Should school leaders be involved in public debates and battles over policy issues? Or should they focus exclusively on taking care of business in their own schools? Why?

6. LaCour states that there are some success stories in public education and that we need to build on them. How can we better market the success stories? And, how can

we replicate the success stories within a district, a state, or a region?

7. What do you perceive to be the key elements needed to change poorly performing schools? What can you do within your school to implement those changes?

Conclusion

Milli Pierce

P ublic schools provide the best hope of educating the millions of children who reside within America's borders. Over five million teachers are employed in this enterprise, along with more than 92,000 principals. This is not the biggest business in the United States, but in many communities the public school system employs more people than any other local business.

Currently, too few children are being educated to work in the technological environment. Manufacturing, computer hardware and software, and biochemical companies, just to name a few, rely on our public schools to prepare their future work force. The question we must ask ourselves is, "Are we doing a good enough job getting all children prepared for the world we live in?" According to the state tests offered in 49 of 50 states, the answer is no. Perhaps the reason for this is that we have been unable to come to consensus around three important questions: What should children know? What should children be able to do? What should children be like when we send them into the world at the end of the twelfth grade?

Anyone using a desktop computer, laptop, or handheld knows about the rapid growth rate in technology. The rate of improvement in hardware seems to double every five years. I owned my first computer in 1984. It had an external disk drive, was too heavy to pick up, and cost over $5,000. Now I have a laptop that has much more memory, weighs three pounds, and cost $1,200. I haven't gotten to the point of using my Palm in lieu of my laptop, but I know I'll be there soon.

We are living in a new world. The Internet has changed our lives forever: there is virtually nothing we cannot learn about people, places, or things within minutes. Who will continue to advance this rapidly expanding knowledge? If our own children do not have the education to do so, employees will be imported from elsewhere.

The jobs for our children reside in this future. What skills and knowledge bases should children know and be able to apply? If we examine school curricula the problem becomes transparent. In the past, educators have taught based on a simplistic approach. For example, the student is taught to "do" mathematics. Then the teacher tries to get the student to apply the knowledge within the discipline, meaning that the student must solve problems based on an algorithm or formula. In some schools students are then taught to apply the knowledge between disciplines—for example, to consider how the mathematics lesson can be used to solve a problem involving science or music. But rarely do students learn to apply knowledge to real-world, predictable problems (those that surface in our everyday lives) and unpredictable problems (those that we have not anticipated but will need to solve). The most challenging and necessary learning is in the realm of these problems. Can schools meet this demand?

At the moment the answer seems too obvious. We are nowhere near where we should be. A look at our middle and high schools tells us much about what we need to know. Thirty-five percent of ninth and tenth graders are reading at fifth- or sixth-grade levels, sometimes less. What should students know? They should know how to read. High school teachers do not teach literacy; that is not what they have been trained to do. A conversation last year with my cousin, who teaches high school mathematics, highlights the problem. I asked her about her biggest challenge. She said she didn't know how to teach reading, and in her estimation her students needed that most. She confirmed what I knew, that literacy is not part of the high school curriculum. If high school students cannot read at grade level, they are not likely to be prepared to compete for positions in a knowledge-based economy.

What students need to know has a direct impact on the principal's role. Expectations for school principals have changed along with demands on K–12 faculty. The principal serving primarily as a manager has been supplanted by the need for the principal to be the leader of instruction. This new world demands principals who know how to identify teacher leaders, build strong instructional teams, enlist leadership within the school community, oversee instruction, and, of course, understand what instruction is needed. Additionally, today's principals must keep apace of curricular reforms and find ways to provide faculty with the professional development necessary for meaningful improvement.

To meet these demands, principals have a plethora of information at their disposal about student performance and teacher competence. Year after year students are tested, providing schools with rich data on what they are learning. However, few principals effectively analyze and use these data. Children are tested all the time, only to have this information used for front-page stories in the local newspaper rather than as a tool to help guide instructional choices. All of these data could easily provide the foundation for teacher professional development, but learning to read and analyze data requires a new set of skills. Principals need to learn how to disaggregate data, determine which students are learning, and help teachers develop effective strategies to overcome student deficiencies. These skills are necessary if schools are going to be able to educate students successfully for a knowledge-based economy.

Principals have huge demands on their time. Perhaps this simple declarative sentence explains why there is such a shortage of principals in the United States. We anticipate losing 40 percent of the nation's principals in the next three years. Accountability has pervaded the schoolhouse without an increase in authority. One principal confided that it took three years to remove an incompetent teacher. In addition, principals work longer hours than they used to. In 1975, the typical school principal worked 40 hours; most now work 60. Longer hours, teacher unions, and difficult community problems have changed the principal's role to one few seek.

Principals are, above all, child advocates. To exercise this role effectively they must know and understand cultural differences among families and faculty. Many communities are divided as much by class as by race. More and more students are migrating to the United States, stratifying communities in ways never imagined 30 years ago. Movement across national borders is an everyday occurrence. Bilingual children populate every U.S. school, where their bilingualism is unfortunately typically seen as a detriment. The principal's role is to provide a socially just and equitable education for every student within the school—not an easy task when the focus is on testing, testing, and more testing. The principal must ensure the education of every child, including children who arrive with their families in search of a better life and those born here who also seek a better life.

In my classes I often ask students about the purpose of schooling, and every year I am forced to reexamine my values and beliefs. Lorraine Monroe, a former New York City principal and a person from whom I have learned much about the principal's role in public schools, uses a phrase that encapsulates my current thinking about the purpose of schooling— namely, that effective schools should transform children's lives. The principal's job is to ensure that every child is seen as a child of promise. No principal should ever allow a teacher to limit a child's promise. I have never met a child who did not want to be valued, respected, and loved. But if children do not have the requisite skills to function adequately in this world, chances are they will not learn to love themselves, nor will they believe others are capable of loving them. Put simply, our society cannot afford to entertain the concept of throwaway children.

The skills principals need are available and accessible; there is no mystery to them. Superintendents, principals, and teacher unions can and must work together to create public schools where all children feel successful and valued. We know everything we need to know about how to do it. But, as Ron Edmonds, pioneer of the "effective schools" movement, has asked, "How do we feel about the fact that we haven't done it so far?"

About the Contributors

Richard F. Elmore is the Gregory R. Anrig Professor of Educational Leadership at the Harvard Graduate School of Education. His research focuses on the effects of federal, state, and local education policy on schools and classrooms. He is currently exploring how schools of different types and in different policy contexts develop a sense of accountability and a capacity to deliver high-quality instruction. Elmore is a Senior Research Fellow with the Consortium for Policy Research in Education (CPRE), a group of universities engaged in research on state and local education policy, funded by the U.S. Department of Education. He is the coauthor of *Restructuring in the Classroom: Teaching, Learning, and School Organization* (with Penelope L. Peterson and Sarah J. McCarthey) and coeditor (with Bruce Fuller) of *Who Chooses, Who Loses? Culture, Institutions, and the Unequal Effects of School Choice*.

Chester E. Finn, Jr., is president of the Thomas B. Fordham Foundation and the John M. Olin Fellow at the Manhattan Institute. He is also a Distinguished Visiting Fellow at Stanford University's Hoover Institution. From 1995 through 1998, he was a Senior Fellow of the Hudson Institute, and he served as founding partner and senior scholar with the Edison Project from 1992 to 1994. With William J. Bennett and John Cribb, Finn authored *The Educated Child: A Parent's Guide from Pre-School through Eighth Grade*. His other publications include *Charter School in Action: Renewing Public Education*, cowritten with Bruno V. Manno and Gregg Vanourek. He was Assistant Secretary for Research and Improvement at the U.S. Department of Education from 1985 to 1988.

Harold L. Hodgkinson is director of the Center for Demographic Policy at the Institute for Educational Leadership in Washington, DC. He is the author of 12 books, three of which have won national awards. Hodgkinson is widely known as an analyst of demographic and educational issues, and he has prepared demographic reports for states, cities, businesses, and nonprofit groups. Recent studies include "Bringing Tomorrow into Focus," "Hispanic Americans: A Look Back, A Look Ahead," and "Immigration in America: The Asian Experience"—all of which are available from the Institute for Educational Leadership. Hodgkinson also served as a fellow at the American Council on Education and as president of the National Training Laboratories.

Nat LaCour is executive vice president of the million-member American Federation of Teachers (AFT), the first person to hold this position. Elected in July 1998, he assists the AFT's president in the day-to-day functions of the union. Prior to his election, LaCour spent 27 years as president of AFT's New Orleans affiliate, the United Teachers of New Orleans. As executive vice president, he has been actively involved in leading AFT's efforts to assist inner-city schools in raising the academic achievement of students. LaCour began his career as a biology teacher in the New Orleans Public Schools.

Robert J. Murphy is director of professional practice and government relations for the Connecticut Education Association. His areas of expertise include emerging trends in education, political action, human and civil rights issues, retirement issues, and professional development.

Gil G. Noam is director of the Program in Afterschool Education and Research (PAER) and an associate professor of education at the Harvard Graduate School of Education. He is also an associate professor of psychology at Harvard Medical School and chief of the Hall-Mercer

Laboratory of Developmental Psychology at McLean Hospital's Child and Adolescent Program. Under his guidance, PAER has been leading the effort to establish the field of afterschool education. Noam has published more than 200 papers, articles, and books in the areas of child and adolescent development, and risk and resiliency in clinical, school, and afterschool settings. He is coauthor of *Afterschool Education: Approaches to an Emerging Field* (with Gina Biancarosa and Nadine Dechausay, Harvard Education Press, 2003).

Pedro A. Noguera is the Judith K. Dimon Professor of Communities and Schools at the Harvard Graduate School of Education. Noguera's research focuses on the ways in which schools respond to social and economic forces within the urban environment. He has engaged in collaborative research with several large urban school districts and has published and lectured on topics such as youth violence, race relations within schools, the potential impact of school choice and vouchers on urban public schools, and secondary issues resulting from desegregation in public schools. Noguera has also done extensive research and published several articles on the role of education in political and social change in the Caribbean. He is author of *The Imperatives of Power: Political Change and the Social Basis of Regime Support in Grenada*.

Gary Orfield, professor of education and social policy at the Harvard Graduate School of Education, studies civil rights, urban policy, and minority opportunity. He is the director of the Harvard Project on School Desegregation and codirector of The Civil Rights Project at Harvard University, which is developing and publishing a new generation of research on multiracial civil rights issues. He is the author and editor of a number of books, including *Racial Inequity in Special Education* (with Daniel J. Losen, Harvard Education Press, 2002).

Milli Pierce is director of the Principals' Center at Harvard University and a member of the faculty of the Harvard Graduate School of Education. Her work focuses on exemplary leadership development for an international body of aspiring and veteran principals and other school leaders. Pierce teaches, advises, and mentors aspiring school leaders and directs the Principals' Center Institutes, which are designed specifically to prepare school leaders for the work of the principalship. Since 1988, she has led the center from being an organization serving local school leaders to one serving a vast group of diverse school leaders from all over the U.S. and abroad. As a former principal and expert in her field, Pierce consults with school districts and facilitates forums and seminars throughout the world.

Douglas B. Reeves is chairman and founder of the Center for Performance Assessment and the International Center for Educational Accountability, a nonprofit organization that works with governmental organizations and school systems to improve standards, assessment, and accountability systems. Reeves has authored seven books, among them a series of three focusing on school reform and accountability, including *Holistic Accountability: Serving Children, Schools, and Communities* and *The Twenty-Minute Learning Connection: The Parent's Guide to Standards and Tests*.

Richard Rothstein is a research associate at the Washington, DC–based Economic Policy Institute and the education columnist at the *New York Times*. He is also an adjunct professor of public policy at Occidental College in Los Angeles and a senior correspondent for *American Prospect* magazine. Rothstein's recent publications include *The Way We Were? Myths and Realities of America's Student Achievement* and *Can Public Schools Learn from Private Schools?* (with Martin Carnoy and Luis Beneviste).

Deborah L. Stapleton, a 2002 Harvard University administrative fellow at the Principals' Center, has more than 20 years of experience in the field of development and fundraising. She is cochair of the National Leadership Academy of the Delta Sigma Theta Sorority and a member of its National Executive Board. She was previously a Leadership NJ Fellow and a National Urban Fellow.

Marcelo M. Suárez-Orozco is the Victor S. Thomas Professor of Education at the Harvard Graduate School of Education, codirector of the Harvard Immigration Project, and chair of the Interfaculty Committee on Latino Studies at Harvard University. Suárez-Orozco's work is in the areas of cultural psychology and psychological anthropology, with a focus on the study of immigration. He is the author of many scholarly essays, books, and edited volumes, the most recent of which are *Children of Immigration* (with Carola Suárez-Orozco) and the six-volume series entitled *Interdisciplinary Perspectives on the New Immigration* (coedited with Carola Suárez-Orozco and Desirée Qin-Hilliard).

Belinda Williams is the former managing director for research and development for the Center for Health, Achievement, Neighborhood, Growth, and Ethnic Studies (CHANGES) at the University of Pennsylvania. She is a former senior research and development specialist at the Northeast and Islands Regional Educational Laboratory at Brown University, as well as director of the Urban Educational Project at Research for Better Schools. A cognitive psychologist with more than 25 years' experience studying the academic achievement patterns of culturally different and poor students in urban districts, Williams is the author of several publications and editor of the recently published *Closing the Achievement Gap: A Vision for Changing Beliefs and Practices.*

Acknowledgements

The Principals' Center is grateful to many organizations and individuals for their assistance in planning, presenting, and participating in Leadership and Policy: An Education Forum. First, we owe a debt of gratitude to the National Education Association (NEA) and its president Robert F. Chase, to the American Federation of Teachers (AFT) and its president Sandra Feldman, and to executive vice president Nat LaCour. The NEA and AFT provided much-needed financial support and assisted the Principals' Center in spreading the word throughout their memberships about the Leadership and Policy Forum. Robert Chase and Nat LaCour also made presentations.

In addition, we owe a debt of gratitude to the Harvard Graduate School of Education faculty members who gave their time to participate: Richard F. Elmore, Pedro A. Noguera, Gil G. Noam, Gary Orfield, Catherine Snow, Marcelo M. Suárez-Orozco, and Charles V. Willie.

Oliver Wendell Holmes said, "One's mind, once stretched by a new idea, never regains its original dimensions." With this in mind, we thank Douglas B. Reeves for stretching our minds and challenging the Principals' Center to develop a forum that would explore reform from a variety of perspectives, from the viewpoint of researchers as well as practitioners. We also are especially grateful to presenters Chester E. Finn, Jr., Harold L. Hodgkinson, Richard Rothstein, Belinda Williams, Janice Williams, Betty Castor, and Anand Vaishnav.

Most important, we want to thank the practitioners who participated on the panels and as members of the audience, contributing not only their voices but also their expertise and firsthand knowledge.

They were pivotal to the forum's success. We extend special thanks to Suzanne Lee, principal of Boston's Josiah Quincy Elementary School, and Linda Nathan, headmaster of the Boston Arts Academy, for their participation. Practitioners are too often left out of discussions about reform policy, yet they are held accountable for implementing those reforms. This forum brought research and practice together so that the participating principals could leave knowing that true educational reform could begin and end in their buildings.

Thanks to the Principals' Center Advisory Board for embracing the idea and helping develop it into the forum. Also, thanks to the Principals' Center staff for their roles in developing and implementing the forum: Betty McNally, assistant director; Angie Yang, Cathy Downey, and Martine Severin, staff assistants; Allison McGrath Borden, teaching assistant; Marlene Pannell, visiting practitioner; Donna Stanton, staff assistant, the International Principals' Center; and former program assistant Mary Kenyatta, who made the initial contacts and organized the forum.

We want to thank the Harvard Graduate School of Education external relations department, which helped publicize the event. And special thanks to the staff of the *Harvard Education Letter*, including Michael Sadowski and David Gordon, who helped shepherd the book to publication.

We thank our families, the families of the practitioners, and the families of the children that we serve for making it all possible. In everything we do, we know that we are building for our children so that they may grow to become all that they can be. Our work is for them.

Finally, we want to thank Roland S. Barth for creating the Principals' Center at the Harvard Graduate School of Education. We are truly indebted to him.

Milli Pierce and Deborah L. Stapleton

The Principals' Center

Founded in 1981, the Principals' Center at Harvard University sup-
ports the personal and professional development of school leaders
through institutes, small interest groups, lectures, and publications.
It is also home to the International Network of Principals' Centers,
which fosters the exchange of ideas and facilitates professional communication among principals' centers and leadership academies
throughout the United States and other countries.

The Principals' Center
Harvard Graduate School of Education
8 Story St., Ground Level
Cambridge, MA 02138
617-495-1825 phone
617-495-5900 fax
principals@gse.harvard.edu
http://www.gse.harvard.edu/~principals/